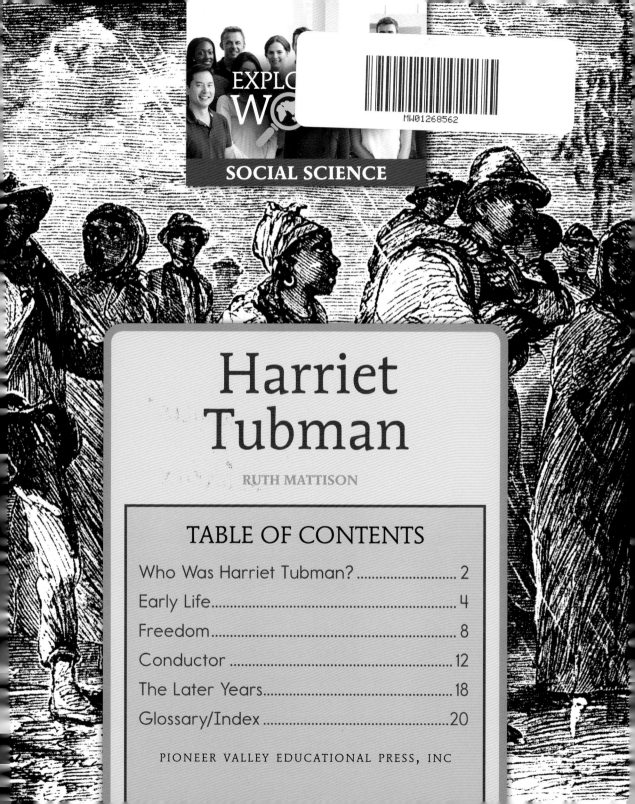

EXPLORING OUR WORLD

SOCIAL SCIENCE

Harriet Tubman

RUTH MATTISON

TABLE OF CONTENTS

PIONEER VALLEY EDUCATIONAL PRESS, INC

WHO WAS HARRIET TUBMAN?

Harriet Tubman was a brave woman
who lived long ago.
She risked her life to help many black slaves
escape from the South to the North
where they could be free.

Keeping the Flame of Freedom Alive

EARLY LIFE

Harriet was born a slave.

Harriet's mother and father were also slaves.

Harriet's parents worked on a large farm called a **plantation**.

Slaves on the plantation had to work very hard to please their **master**.

The master was the man who owned the plantation.

Slaves could be sold to another master.

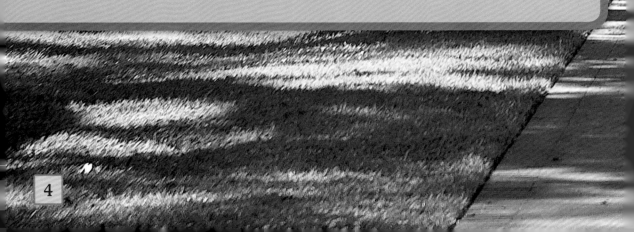

Plantations often grew crops such as cotton.
Here, slaves are putting the cotton into a cotton gin.

5

When Harriet was about five years old,
she had to start working on the plantation.
At first she worked in the master's house.
When she got older, she was sent
outside to work on the farm.
She drove a wagon, plowed fields,
and moved heavy logs.

One day, Harriet suffered a head injury.
Because she was a slave,
Harriet was not taken to a doctor.

Two days later, even though she was still badly hurt, Harriet had to go back to work. Harriet had problems from this head **wound** for the rest of her life.

FREEDOM

Harriet married a man
named John Tubman.
John was not a slave.
He was a free black man.

Then Harriet became ill.

She was worried that she would be sold

to another master so she decided

to run away. She traveled to the North

where she thought she could find freedom.

Harriet didn't have a map

to go north. Instead she followed

the North Star.

She hid during the day and walked at night.

Harriet met people along the way
who helped her.
They gave her food to eat
and hid her from people
who were trying to catch her.

Finally, after traveling for several weeks,
Harriet reached the northern city
of Philadelphia.

Harriet was very happy to reach freedom.

MORE TO EXPLORE

The Underground Railroad
was a secret group of
routes that black slaves
used to escape from
the South to the North.

MORE TO EXPLORE

This is what Harriet said about how it felt to reach the North: "When I found I had crossed that line, I looked at my hands to see if I was the same person. There was such a glory over everything; the sun came like gold through the trees, and over the fields, and I felt like I was in Heaven."

CONDUCTOR

Harriet wanted to help her family
and other slaves escape to freedom.
She began to make trips
back to the South,
which was very dangerous.
If caught, she would have been sent back
to her master.

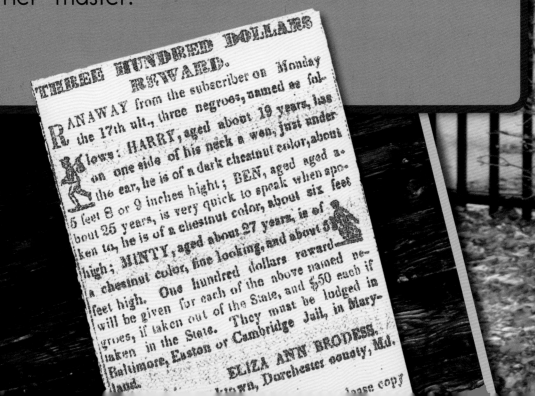

THREE HUNDRED DOLLARS
REWARD.

RANAWAY from the subscriber on Monday
the 17th ult., three negroes, named as fol-
lows: HARRY, aged about 19 years, has
on one side of his neck a wen, just under
the ear, he is of a dark chestnut color, about
5 feet 8 or 9 inches hight; BEN, aged a-
bout 25 years, is very quick to speak when spo-
ken to, he is of a chestnut color, about six feet
high; MINTY, aged about 27 years, is of
a chestnut color, fine looking, and about 5
feet high. One hundred dollars reward
will be given for each of the above named negroes, if taken out of the State, and $50 each if
taken in the State. They must be lodged in
Baltimore, Easton or Cambridge Jail, in Maryland.

ELIZA ANN BRODESS,
————town, Dorchester county, Md,

lease copy

During her trips, she found people who would help hide runaway slaves. Since Harriet would **guide** the people to freedom, she was called a "**conductor**" of the Underground Railroad.

For 11 years, Harriet traveled from the North to the South, helping her family and other slaves escape.

MORE TO EXPLORE

Many homes along the Underground Railroad route were used as safe places for escaped slaves to stay, such as this home in Charlemont, Massachusetts.

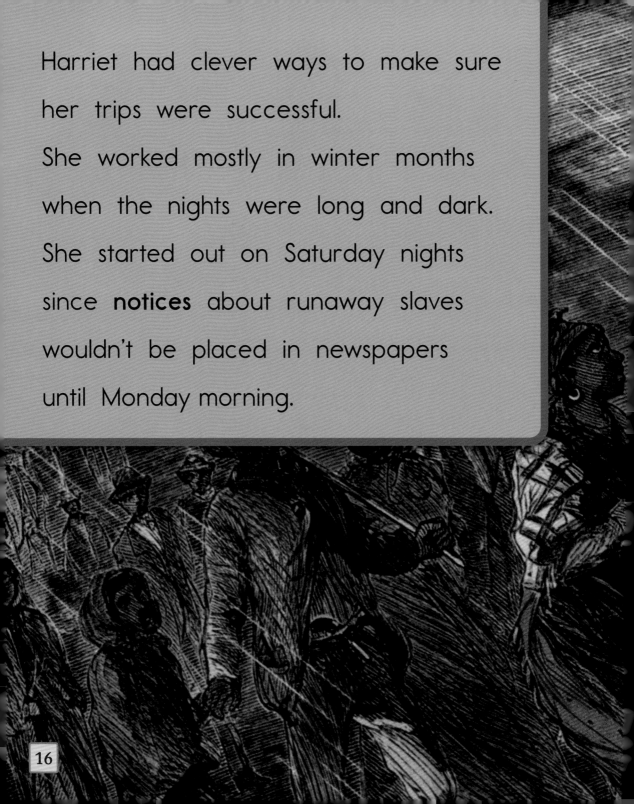

Harriet had clever ways to make sure her trips were successful.

She worked mostly in winter months when the nights were long and dark.

She started out on Saturday nights since **notices** about runaway slaves wouldn't be placed in newspapers until Monday morning.

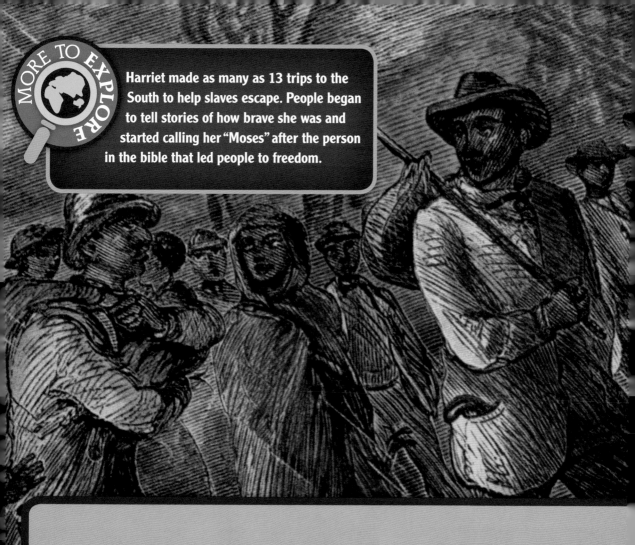

MORE TO EXPLORE

Harriet made as many as 13 trips to the South to help slaves escape. People began to tell stories of how brave she was and started calling her "Moses" after the person in the bible that led people to freedom.

Once on a train, she saw her old master.

Everyone knew Harriet could not read,

so she picked up a newspaper

and pretended to read it.

The man did not notice her.

THE LATER YEARS

In 1859, Harriet bought a farm in New York where she brought her family and friends to live.

There was a war between the North and the South. The North wanted the slaves to be free. Harriet helped the North by working as a cook and a nurse.

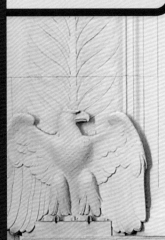

18

The war went on for a long time.
Finally the North won the war,
and the slaves were free.
The law changed so slaves no longer
had to work for a master.
Now they could live and work
wherever they chose.

After the war, Harriet went
back to New York.
For the rest of her life,
Harriet continued to help black men
and women make new lives
as free people.

19

1858

Harriet shares details of
the Underground Railroad
with John Brown, who planned raids
on slaveholders in Harpers Ferry, VA

1860

Harriet conducts her last
rescue mission

1863

Harriet serves as a cook, nurse,
and leader in the American Civil War

1913

Harriet dies at her farm in Auburn, NY

HARRIET TUBMAN
TIME LINE

1820
Harriet is born to slave parents

1844
Harriet marries a free black man named John Tubman

1849
Harriet escapes from the plantation in Maryland and travels to Philadelphia

1850
Harriet begins to guide other slaves to freedom

GLOSSARY

conductor
someone in charge of
the people on a train

guide
someone who leads others

master
a person who owns slaves

notices
written or printed announcements

plantation
a large farm worked by
slaves or workers

wound
a cut or break to the skin

INDEX